INCREDIBLE INVENTORS

THE WRIGHT BROTHERS AND THE AIRPLANE

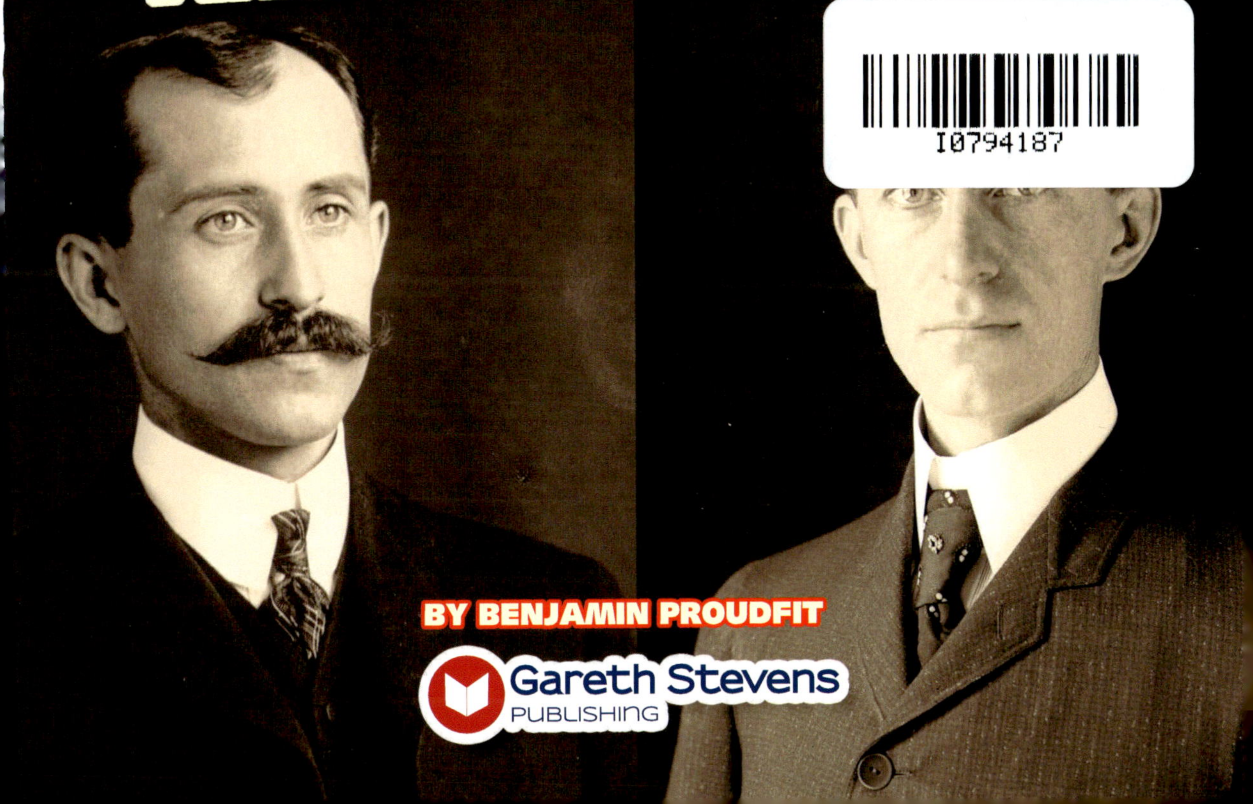

BY BENJAMIN PROUDFIT

Gareth Stevens PUBLISHING

Please visit our website, www.garethstevens.com. For a free color catalog of all our high-quality books, call toll free 1-800-542-2595 or fax 1-877-542-2596.

Library of Congress Cataloging-in-Publication Data

Names: Proudfit, Benjamin, author.
Title: The Wright brothers and the airplane / Benjamin Proudfit.
Description: New York : Gareth Stevens Publishing, [2023] | Series: Incredible inventors | Includes index.
Identifiers: LCCN 2021036617 (print) | LCCN 2021036618 (ebook) | ISBN 9781538276662 (set) | ISBN 9781538276679 (library binding) | ISBN 9781538276655 (paperback) | ISBN 9781538276686 (ebook)
Subjects: LCSH: Wright, Wilbur, 1867-1912–Juvenile literature. | Wright, Orville, 1871-1948–Juvenile literature. | Aeronautics–United States–Biography–Juvenile literature. | Inventors–United States–Biography–Juvenile literature.
Classification: LCC TL540.W7 P76 2023 (print) | LCC TL540.W7 (ebook) | DDC 629.130092/273–dc23
LC record available at https://lccn.loc.gov/2021036617
LC ebook record available at https://lccn.loc.gov/2021036618

Published in 2023 by
Gareth Stevens Publishing
111 East 14th Street, Suite 349
New York, NY 10003

Designer: Rachel Rising
Editor: Kristen Nelson

Photo credits: Cover, p. 1 (Orville Wright)/Libary of Congress; Cover, p. 1 (Wilbur Wright)/Libary of Congress; pp. 3-24 Zavadskyi Ihor/Shutterstock.com; pp. 3-24 Lukasz Szwaj/Shutterstock.com; p. 5 https://commons.wikimedia.org/wiki/File:Young_Orville_Wright.jpg; p. 5 https://commons.wikimedia.org/wiki/File:Wilbur_Wright_child.jpg; p. 7 https://en.wikipedia.org/wiki/File:Wright_Cycle_Company_Offices.jpg; p. 9 Everett Collection/Shutterstock.com; p. 11 https://en.wikipedia.org/wiki/File:Wright_brothers_engine_17.jpg; p. 13 Chansak Joe/Shutterstock.com; p. 15 https://commons.wikimedia.org/wiki/File:Wright_First_Flight_1903Dec17_(full_restore_115).jpg; pp. 17, 19 Everett Collection/Shutterstock.com; p. 20 Natata/Shutterstock.com.

Printed in the United States of America

CPSIA compliance information: Batch #CSGS23: For further information contact Gareth Stevens, New York, New York at 1-800-542-2595.

CONTENTS

Boldface words appear in the glossary.

The Flight Brothers

Wilbur Wright was born on April 16, 1867, in Indiana. Orville was born August 19, 1871, in Ohio. They were interested in flight even as children. They played with kites and even had a toy helicopter. The brothers were close to one another.

WILBUR WRIGHT

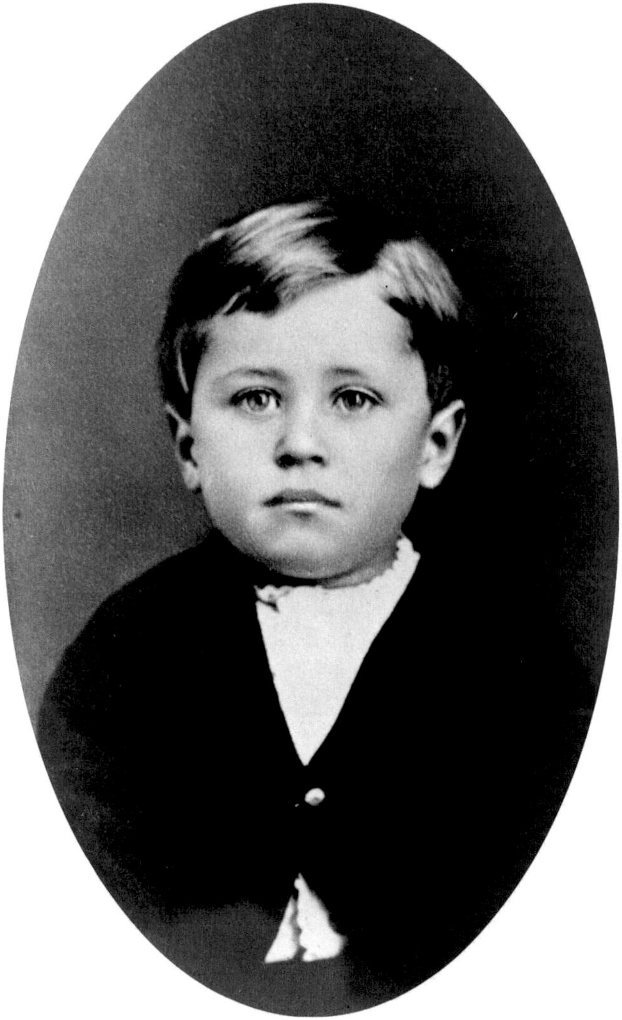

ORVILLE WRIGHT

Orville became a great bicyclist. Wilbur was good at doing **research**. Together, they opened a bicycle shop in 1892. They began to build their own bicycles. This **experience** and their scientific study prepared them for their path into flight.

THE WRIGHT CYCLE CO.

Gliders

Before the Wrights, many people were working on gliders. These aircraft have wings but no **engine**. In 1900, the brothers built their first glider. Wilbur and Orville broke the record for the longest glider flight in 1902.

Adding Power

The Wrights also started working on an aircraft powered by an engine. At the time, no engine was lightweight enough. They **designed** one! They also invented a **propeller** to aid the airplane's flight. It was the first of its kind.

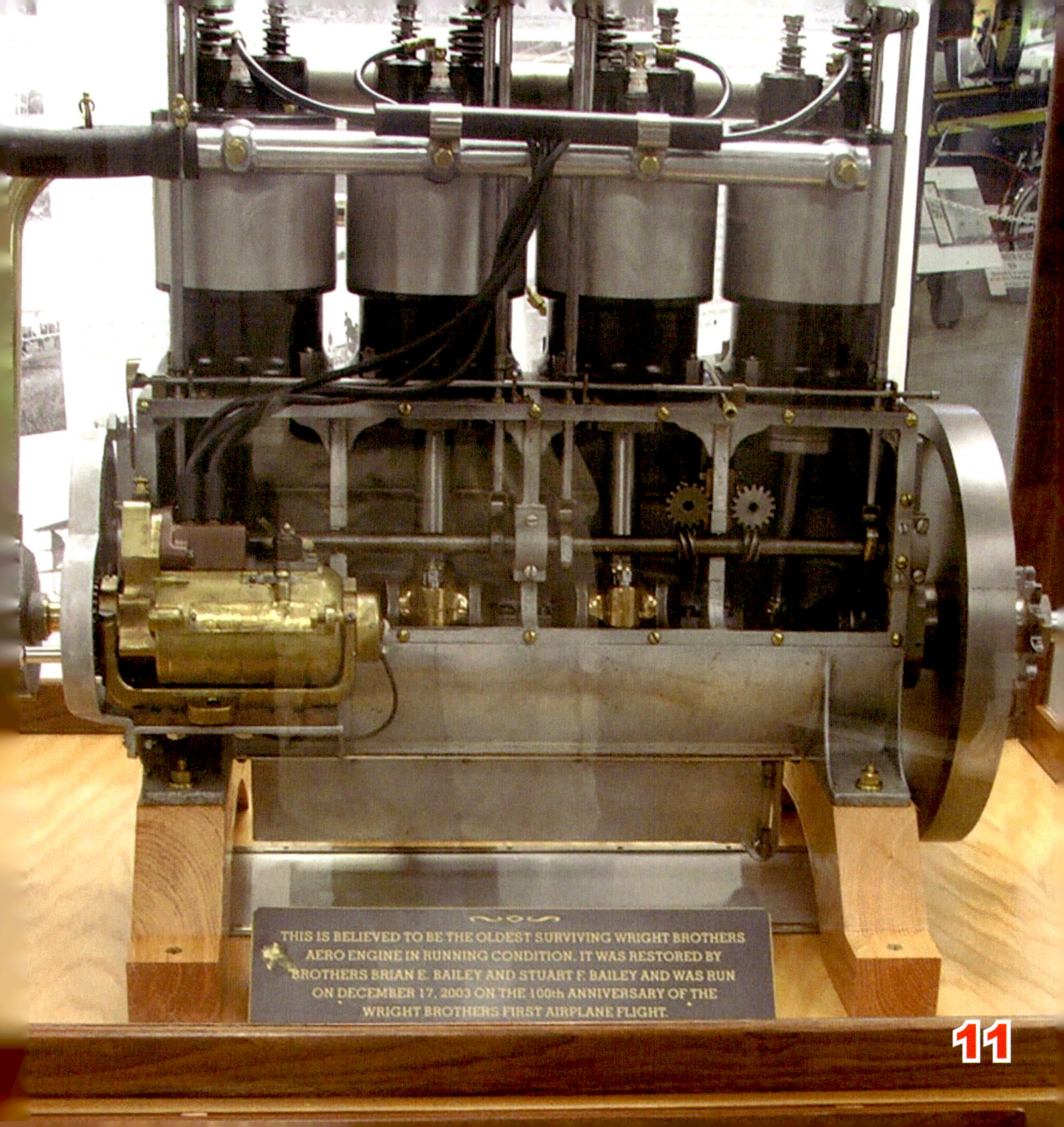
THIS IS BELIEVED TO BE THE OLDEST SURVIVING WRIGHT BROTHERS
AERO ENGINE IN RUNNING CONDITION. IT WAS RESTORED BY
BROTHERS BRIAN E. BAILEY AND STUART F. BAILEY AND WAS RUN
ON DECEMBER 17, 2003 ON THE 100th ANNIVERSARY OF THE
WRIGHT BROTHERS FIRST AIRPLANE FLIGHT.

First Flight

On December 14, 1903, the aircraft Orville and Wilbur built was ready to test. It was called *Flyer I*. The flight would take place in Kitty Hawk, North Carolina. Wilbur won the coin toss to fly first. He **piloted** the plane straight into the sand!

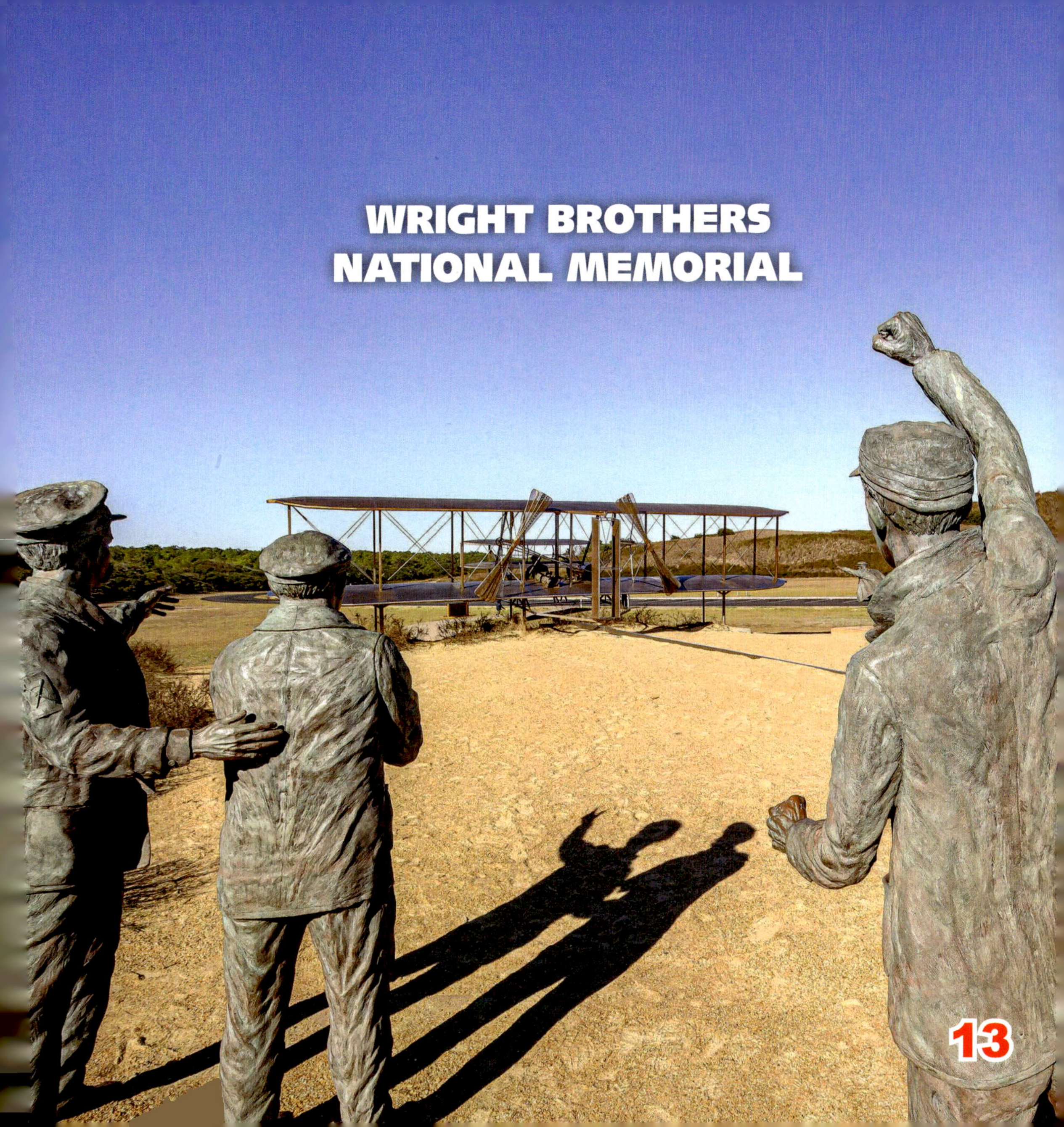
WRIGHT BROTHERS
NATIONAL MEMORIAL

They fixed the plane, and now it was Orville's turn to fly. On December 17, 1903, he flew 120 feet (36.6 m)! It was the first powered airplane flight. Later that day, Wilbur flew for just under a minute and traveled 852 feet (259.7 m).

Next Steps

The Wright brothers continued to work on their aircraft. They went back to Dayton, Ohio, to do more testing. Wilbur and Orville started using a more powerful engine. By 1905, they were able to fly for more than 30 minutes and bring a passenger aboard!

The brothers' success earned them a deal with the U.S. Army in 1909. In 1912, however, Wilbur became sick and died. Orville continued working in **aeronautics**. He was part of the group that became today's National Aeronautics and Space Administration (NASA).

Known Today

Orville died on January 30, 1948. Others had flown before them, but the Wright brothers were the first to power a plane and fly it. This started the age of the airplane! Today, their accomplishments continue to be honored.

TIMELINE

April 16, 1867
Wilbur Wright is born.

August 19, 1871
Orville Wright is born.

1892
The brothers open a bicycle shop.

1900
They build their first glider.

1902
They break the record for the longest glider flight.

December 14, 1903
Wilbur tries to fly *Flyer I*.

December 17, 1903
The Wright brothers achieve the first powered aircraft flight.

1909
They sell a plane to the U.S. Army.

1912
Wilbur dies.

1948
Orville dies.

GLOSSARY

aeronautics: the science of aircraft and how they fly

design: to create the plan or shape of something

engine: a machine that makes power

experience: the process of doing and seeing things and of having things happen to you

pilot: to fly a plane

propeller: paddle-like parts on a plane that spin to move the plane forward

research: studying to find something new

FOR MORE INFORMATION

BOOKS

Hernandez, Marissa. *The Wright Brothers*. Huntington Beach, CA: Teacher Created Materials, 2019.

Koestler-Grack, Rachel A. *Airplanes from Then to Now*. Mankato, MN: Amicus/Amicus Ink, 2021.

WEBSITES

History of Flight

www.grc.nasa.gov/www/k-12/UEET/StudentSite/historyofflight.html

Follow the timeline on this NASA website and learn about the history of flight.

Taking Flight with the Wright Brothers

kids.nationalgeographic.com/history/article/wright-brothers

Find out even more about the Wright Brothers here.

Publisher's note to educators and parents: Our editors have carefully reviewed these websites to ensure that they are suitable for students. Many websites change frequently, however, and we cannot guarantee that a site's future contents will continue to meet our high standards of quality and educational value. Be advised that students should be closely supervised whenever they access the internet.

INDEX